Communion of the Sick

LITURGICAL PRESS
Collegeville, Minnesota

litpress.org

The rites found in this edition of *Communion of the Sick* are taken from chapter two of the ritual book, *Holy Communion and Worship of the Eucharistic Mystery outside Mass*, which provides the rites used by extraordinary ministers of Holy Communion when administering Communion and Viaticum to the sick. Along with *The Order of the Anointing of the Sick and of their Pastoral Care*, the ritual book used by a priest or deacon when administering Holy Communion and Viaticum to the sick, this ritual book represents a careful reworking for English-speaking countries of revisions published since the Second Vatican Council. The numbers which appear to the left of various paragraphs are from the full ritual book. For the convenience of the minister, this book also compiles various ritual options found elsewhere in the full ritual book, which are noted with a "cf." notation.

The minister should be thoroughly familiar with the introduction, "Holy Communion Outside Mass" (pages 8–14) and all the options given in the rites.

Excerpts from the *Lectionary for Mass for Use in the Dioceses of the United States, second edition* Copyright ©1970, 1986, 1992, 1998, 2001 Confraternity of Christian Doctrine, Inc., Washington, D.C. All rights reserved. No part of this work may be reproduced or transmitted in any form or by any means, electronic or mechanical, including photocopying, recording, or by any information storage and retrieval system, without permission in writing from the copyright owner.

The English translation of Psalm responses, some Alleluia and Gospel verses, some Summaries, and the Titles and Conclusion of the Readings from *Lectionary for Mass* © 1969, 1981, 1997, International Commission on English in the Liturgy Corporation (ICEL); excerpts from the English translation of *The Roman Missal* © 2010, ICEL; excerpts from the English translation of *Holy Communion and Worship of the Eucharistic Mystery outside Mass* © 2020, ICEL; excerpts from the English translation of *The Order of the Anointing of the Sick and of their Pastoral Care* © 2020, ICEL. All rights reserved.

Commentaries on the Readings from Scripture © 2012, 2024, by Order of Saint Benedict, Collegeville, Minnesota.

Published with the approval of the Committee on Divine Worship, United States Conference of Catholic Bishops. August 12, 2024.

© 2024 by Order of Saint Benedict, Collegeville, Minnesota. All rights reserved. Printed in the United States of America.

ISBN 978-0-8146-8970-7

CONTENTS

PRAYER OF PREPARATION 5

PREFACE 6

INTRODUCTION
(HOLY COMMUNION OUTSIDE MASS) 8

ADMINISTRATION OF COMMUNION AND VIATICUM TO THE SICK BY AN EXTRAORDINARY MINISTER

THE ORDINARY RITE OF COMMUNION OF THE SICK

- Outline of the Rite 16
- The Introductory Rites 17
- The Shorter Reading of the Word of God 20
- Holy Communion 21
- The Concluding Rites 24

A SHORTER RITE OF COMMUNION OF THE SICK

- Outline of the Rite 26
- The Introductory Rites 27
- Holy Communion 28
- The Concluding Rites 29

VIATICUM

- Outline of the Rite 32
- The Introductory Rites 33
- The Shorter Reading of the Word of God 37
- The Profession of Baptismal Faith 39
- Prayer for the Sick Person 40
- Viaticum 41
- The Concluding Rites 42

APPENDIX

- Additional Readings from Sacred Scripture 44
- Commentary on the Readings from Sacred Scripture 48
- Responsorial Psalms 52

PRAYER OF PREPARATION FOR THE MINISTER

Almighty God, Father of our Lord Jesus Christ, you are the Father of mercies and the God of all consolation. You comfort us in all our afflictions and thus enable us to comfort those who are in trouble, with the same consolation we receive from you.

God of compassion, fill me with the power of your Word and the love of your Holy Spirit as I visit your suffering sons and daughters. Help me so that I may worthily and gracefully share your sacred presence with those who await your coming to them. May the Body and Blood of your Son Jesus Christ heal and comfort us, deepen our faith, and strengthen our hope in the imperishable inheritance you have promised to those who seek you.

Father, I pray to you for myself and for those I visit, in the saving name of Jesus, our risen Lord, who lives and reigns with you and the Holy Spirit, now and forever. Amen.

PREFACE

Communion of the Sick is a classic resource for parishes because it contains—in a portable and easy-to-follow format—the rites needed by every extraordinary minister of Holy Communion in visiting and bringing Communion to the sick. Nevertheless, although structured and designed primarily for their use and at their request, we believe others who wish to visit and pray with the sick will find help here. And many sick or confined persons will benefit from having this book for their prayer as well.

Communion of the Sick includes the official instructions, rites, and texts for ordinary "Communion calls" to the sick and confined. This includes an "Ordinary Rite," a "Shorter Rite" (useful when making multiple visits, as in a hospital), and the rite for an extraordinary minister to use when administering Viaticum (Communion in preparation for death). Since the Second Vatican Council, these rites have been revised several times, and are now presented here as found in chapter two of *Holy Communion and Worship of the Eucharistic Mystery outside Mass*.

An important hallmark of these rites since Vatican II is that they are essentially pastoral, allowing for flexibility by ministers and a variety of ritual options to choose from as they accompany those who are sick. To assist ministers in navigating this variety, *Communion of the Sick* compiles these options, which otherwise appear throughout the full ritual book, within the rites themselves. Additionally, for ease of use, a rich selection of readings is provided in both the Ordinary Rite and Viaticum, but ministers are free to choose readings from either set, from the appendix (see below), or from the Sunday or weekday readings.

Additional features have been included in the appendix beginning on page 44, offering ministers some of the help they have requested:

1. As noted above, additional readings from Sacred Scripture, to provide an even wider variety of texts. The Church since Vatican II has desired a broad selection of Scripture readings.

2. Brief commentaries in the form of meditations follow. They are lettered A to L corresponding to the Scripture reading of the same letter. These meditations may be used to help pray with the readings and to enter into pastoral conversations.

3. Five Psalms have been included at the end of the book. The minister's discretion will determine how one or another Psalm may be used—after listening to a Scripture reading, as a prayer to conclude the visit, or perhaps as a preparation for the rite of Communion.

Our prayerful hope is that many compassionate members of Christ's body, with or without professional preparation as ministers, will find this booklet helpful for themselves and for those they visit in the Lord. To him be glory and praise forever.

HOLY COMMUNION OUTSIDE MASS

INTRODUCTION

I. The Relationships That Exist between Communion outside Mass and the Sacrifice

13. Sacramental Communion received within Mass is the more perfect participation in the Eucharistic Celebration. The Eucharistic sign is expressed more clearly, when the faithful receive the Body of the Lord after the Communion of the Priest, from the same Sacrifice.[1] Therefore recently made bread should be consecrated in every Eucharistic Celebration for the Communion of the faithful.

14. The faithful should be encouraged to receive Communion during the Eucharistic Celebration itself.

Priests, however, should not refuse to give Holy Communion to the faithful who for a just cause seek it, even outside Mass.[2]

In fact, it is fitting that those who are prevented from being present in the Eucharistic community should be diligently refreshed by the Eucharist, and in this way they may

---

[1] Cf. Second Vatican Council, Constitution on the Sacred Liturgy, *Sacrosanctum Concilium*, no. 55: *Acta Apostolicæ Sedis* 56 (1964), p. 115.

[2] Cf. Sacred Congregation of Rites, Instruction *Eucharisticum mysterium*, no. 33a: *Acta Apostolicæ Sedis* 59 (1967), pp. 559–560.

feel themselves united, not only with the Sacrifice of the Lord but also with the community itself, and supported by the love of their brothers and sisters.

Pastors of souls should take care that the sick and aged, even if not gravely sick or in imminent danger of death, should be given the opportunity to receive the Eucharist frequently, even, insofar as possible, daily, especially during Easter Time. Furthermore, it is permitted to administer the Eucharist under the species of wine alone, to those who are unable to receive under the species of bread.[3]

15. The faithful are to be carefully taught that, even when they receive Communion outside the celebration of Mass, they are intimately united with the Sacrifice which perpetuates the Sacrifice of the Cross, and they are participants in that sacred banquet in which, "by Communion in the Body and Blood of the Lord, the People of God participates in the blessings of the Paschal Sacrifice, renews the New Covenant made once by God with men in the Blood of Christ, and in faith and hope prefigures and anticipates the eschatological banquet in the Kingdom of the Father, proclaiming the Death of the Lord until he comes."[4]

II. The Time for Administering Holy Communion outside Mass

16. Holy Communion may be given outside Mass on any day and at any time of the day. It is proper, however, to determine times for the distribution of Holy Communion, bearing in mind the convenience of the faithful, so that the sacred celebration may be enacted in a fuller form, for the greater spiritual benefit of the faithful.

---

[3] Cf. *ibidem*, nos. 40–41: *loc. cit.*, pp. 562–563.
[4] *Ibidem*, no. 3a: *loc. cit.*, pp. 541–542.

Nevertheless:

a) on Thursday of Holy Week, Holy Communion may be distributed only during Mass; it may, however, be brought to the sick at any time of the day;

b) on Good Friday of the Passion of the Lord, Holy Communion is distributed only during the celebration of the Passion of the Lord; but it may, however, be brought to the sick, who cannot take part in the celebration, at any time of the day;

c) on Holy Saturday, Holy Communion may be given only as Viaticum.[5]

III. The Minister of Holy Communion

17. It is first of all for the Priest or Deacon to administer Holy Communion to the faithful who ask for it.[6] It is in every way proper, therefore, that they should give part of their time to the performance of this ministry, according to the needs of the faithful.

Moreover, it is for a duly instituted acolyte, as an extraordinary minister, to give Holy Communion whenever there is no Priest or Deacon, either because of sickness, old age, or because they are prevented by pastoral duties or the number of faithful coming to the holy table is so great that the celebration of the Mass or other sacred celebration may be greatly prolonged.[7]

The local Ordinary may give the faculty of distributing Holy Communion to other extraordinary ministers, when-

---

[5] Cf. *Missale Romanum, editio typica tertia emendata* (2008), *Ad Missam vespertinam*, no. 4; *Celebratio Passionis Domini*, no. 2; *Sabbato sancto*, no. 3.

[6] Cf. Sacred Congregation of Rites, Instruction *Eucharisticum mysterium*, no. 31: *Acta Apostolicæ Sedis* 59 (1967), pp. 557–558.

[7] Cf. Paul VI, Apostolic Letter *Ministeria quædam*, August 15, 1972, no. VI: *Acta Apostolicæ Sedis* 64 (1972), p. 532.

ever it may seem necessary for the pastoral benefit of the faithful, and a Priest or Deacon or acolyte is not available.[8]

IV. The Place for Distributing Communion outside Mass

18. The place in which Holy Communion is normally given outside Mass is a church or oratory in which the Eucharist is regularly celebrated or reserved, or a church or oratory or other place in which the local community habitually comes together for the liturgical assembly on Sundays or other days. However, Holy Communion may be given in other places, not excluding private houses, when the sick, prisoners, or others involved cannot leave the place without danger or grave difficulty.

V. Norms Governing the Distribution of Holy Communion

19. When Holy Communion is administered in a church or oratory, a corporal should be placed on the altar, which is already covered with a cloth; two candles should be lit, as a sign of veneration and of the festive banquet.[9] A paten should be used.

But when Holy Communion is administered in other places, a suitable table is prepared, covered with a cloth; candles should also be provided.

20. The minister of Holy Communion, if he is a Priest or Deacon, should be vested in an alb, or a surplice over a cassock, and should wear a stole.

---

[8] Cf. Sacred Congregation for the Discipline of the Sacraments, Instruction *Immensæ caritatis*, January 29, 1973, 1, I and II: *Acta Apostolicæ Sedis* 65 (1973), pp. 265–266.

[9] Cf. *Missale Romanum, editio typica tertia emendata* (2008), *Institutio generalis*, no. 307.

Other ministers should wear either the liturgical vesture traditional in their region or vesture which is not unsuitable for this ministry and is approved by the Ordinary.

The Eucharist for administering Communion outside the church should be carried in a pyx or other closed vessel, with such coverings and in such a manner as is appropriate to the place.

21. In distributing Holy Communion the custom of placing a particle of consecrated bread on the tongue of the communicant is to be observed, because it is based on a tradition of several centuries.

However, the Conferences of Bishops may determine, when their decisions have been confirmed by the Apostolic See, that in their jurisdiction, Holy Communion may be distributed by placing the consecrated bread in the hands of the faithful, provided that due care is taken that no lack of reverence or false opinions about the Most Holy Eucharist should insinuate themselves into the minds of the faithful.[10]

Moreover, the faithful should be taught that Jesus Christ is Lord and Savior and that, present in the sacramental species, he should be given the same worship or adoration that is due to God.[11]

In either case, Communion should be given by the competent minister, who shows the particle of consecrated bread to the communicant and gives it to him (her), saying the words, The Body of Christ, to which the communicant replies, Amen.

---

[10] Cf. Sacred Congregation for Divine Worship, Instruction *Memoriale Domini*, May 29, 1969: *Acta Apostolicæ Sedis* 61 (1969), pp. 541–555.

[11] Cf. Sacred Congregation for the Discipline of the Sacraments, Instruction *Immensæ caritatis*, January 29, 1973, no. 4: *Acta Apostolicæ Sedis* 65 (1973), p. 270.

With regard to what pertains to the distribution of Holy Communion under the species of wine, the liturgical norms should be observed exactly.[12]

22. Fragments that may remain after Communion should be reverently collected and placed in a pyx or put into a vessel with water.

Similarly, if Communion is administered under the species of wine, the chalice or other vessel used for this purpose should be washed with water.

The water used for the ablutions may be either drunk or poured out in an appropriate place.

VI. Dispositions for Receiving Holy Communion

23. The Eucharist, which continuously represents the Paschal Mystery of Christ in the midst of humanity, is the fount of all grace and of the remission of sins. Nevertheless, those who intend to receive the Body of the Lord, should come to it with clean consciences and properly disposed souls, so that they may harvest the fruits of the paschal Sacrament.

The Church therefore teaches "that no one conscious of mortal sin in themselves, however contrite they feel themselves to be, should receive the Holy Eucharist without previous sacramental confession."[13] If there is a serious reason and no opportunity for confession, they should make

---

[12] Cf. *Missale Romanum, editio typica tertia emendata* (2008), *Institutio generalis*, no. 283; cf. Sacred Congregation for Divine Worship, Instruction *Sacramentali Communione*, June 29, 1970, no. 6: *Acta Apostolicæ Sedis* 62 (1970), pp. 665–666.

[13] Cf. Council of Trent, Session XIII, *Decretum de ss. Eucharistiæ sacramento*, cap. 7: Denzinger-Schönmetzer 1646–1647; *ibidem*, Session XIV, *Canones de sacramento Pœnitentiæ*, can. 9: Denzinger-Schönmetzer 1709; Sacred Congregation for the Doctrine of the Faith, *Pastoral Norms for the Administration of General Sacramental Absolution*, June 16, 1972, Introduction and no. VI: *Acta Apostolicæ Sedis* 64 (1972), pp. 510 and 512.

an act of perfect contrition with the intention of confessing individually, as soon as possible, the mortal sins that they cannot confess at present.

It is desirable that those who are accustomed to communicate daily or quite often go to the Sacrament of Penance at regular intervals, depending on their circumstances.

Moreover, the faithful should look on the Eucharist as an antidote that frees them from daily faults and preserves them from mortal sins; in addition, they should understand the right way to use the penitential parts of the liturgy, especially of the Mass.[14]

24. Communicants should not receive the Sacrament unless they have fasted for at least one hour from food and drink, with the sole exceptions of water and medicine.

The elderly and those suffering from any kind of infirmity, as well as those who take care of such persons, may receive the Most Holy Eucharist even if they have consumed something within the hour before.[15]

25. Union with Christ, to which the Sacrament itself is directed, should be extended to the whole Christian life, so that the Christian faithful, continually contemplating the gift they have received, live their daily lives under the guidance of the Holy Spirit, as an act of thanksgiving, and bring forth more abundantly the fruits of charity.

In order that they may more easily continue the act of thanksgiving which is offered to God in a splendid way in the Mass, it is recommended that all who have been refreshed in Holy Communion should continue in prayer for a certain period of time.[16]

---

[14] Cf. Sacred Congregation of Rites, Instruction *Eucharisticum mysterium*, no. 35: *Acta Apostolicæ Sedis* 59 (1967), p. 561.

[15] Cf. *Code of Canon Law*, can. 919 §§ 1 and 3.

[16] Cf. Sacred Congregation of Rites, Instruction *Eucharisticum mysterium*, no. 38: *Acta Apostolicæ Sedis* 59 (1967), p. 562.

ADMINISTRATION OF COMMUNION AND VIATICUM TO THE SICK BY AN EXTRAORDINARY MINISTER

54. A Priest or Deacon administers Holy Communion and Viaticum to the sick according to the rites in *The Order of the Anointing of the Sick and of their Pastoral Care*. When, however, the Most Holy Eucharist is brought to the sick by an acolyte or an extraordinary minister of Holy Communion deputed in accordance with the norm of law, the rites that follow are to be observed.

55. It is permitted to administer the Eucharist under the species of wine alone to those who are unable to receive it under the species of bread.

The Blood of the Lord must be carried to the sick person in a vessel so closed as to avoid completely any danger of spillage. In administering the Sacrament, however, the more appropriate manner should be chosen, in each case, from those proposed for distributing Communion under both kinds. When Communion is completed, if any of the Most Precious Blood remains, it should be consumed by the minister, who should also take care of the necessary purifications.

OUTLINE OF THE ORDINARY RITE OF COMMUNION OF THE SICK

THE INTRODUCTORY RITES

THE SHORTER READING OF THE WORD OF GOD

HOLY COMMUNION

THE CONCLUDING RITES

THE ORDINARY RITE OF COMMUNION OF THE SICK

The Introductory Rites

56. Wearing vestments appropriate for this ministry (cf. no. 20), after approaching the sick person, the minister warmly greets them and the others present, using, if appropriate, the greeting:

A **Peace to this house and all here.**

Other words from Sacred Scripture, with which the faithful are customarily greeted, may also be used (cf. nos. 27 and 189):

> [If using a greeting with a response, the minister may find it pastorally helpful to add the response to the end of the greeting, and then invite all to respond.]

B **Bless the Lord, brothers and sisters,**
who in his goodness invites us (you)
to the table of the Body of Christ.

> All: Blessed be God for ever.

C **Grace to you and peace from God our Father**
and the Lord Jesus Christ.

> All: Blessed be the God and Father of our Lord Jesus Christ.

Then, after placing the Sacrament on a table, the minister and all present adore it.

57. The minister invites the sick person and others present to take part in the Penitential Act:

> **Brethren (Brothers and sisters), let us acknowledge our sins,**
> **and so prepare ourselves to participate in this sacred celebration.**

A brief pause for silence follows. Then all recite together the I confess:

A I confess to almighty God
and to you, my brothers and sisters,
that I have greatly sinned,
in my thoughts and in my words,
in what I have done and in what I have failed to do,

And, striking their breast, they say:

through my fault, through my fault,
through my most grievous fault;

Then they continue:

therefore I ask blessed Mary ever-Virgin,
all the Angels and Saints
and you, my brothers and sisters,
to pray for me to the Lord our God.

Other optional formulas of the Penitential Act (cf. nos. 190–191):

B Minister: **Have mercy on us, O Lord.**
All: For we have sinned against you.

Minister: **Show us, O Lord, your mercy.**
All: And grant us your salvation.

C Minister: **You gained salvation for us by your Paschal Mystery:
Lord, have mercy**
Or: **Kyrie, eleison.**

All: Lord, have mercy.
Or: Kyrie, eleison.

Minister: **You never cease to renew among us the wonders of your Passion:
Christ, have mercy.**
Or: **Christe, eleison.**

All: Christ, have mercy.
Or: Christe, eleison.

Minister: **You make us sharers in your Paschal Sacrifice through the reception of your Body:
Lord, have mercy.**
Or: **Kyrie, eleison.**

All: Lord, have mercy.
Or: Kyrie, eleison.

The minister concludes:

May almighty God have mercy on us, forgive us our sins, and bring us to everlasting life.

All reply: Amen.

The Shorter Reading of the Word of God

58. Then, a short text of Sacred Scripture, for example from those indicated below (cf. no. 71), may be read as appropriate by one of those present or by the minister.

[Readings may also be chosen from those that appear beginning on page 37 (which are suitable for the Ordinary Rite of Communion of the Sick as well as Viaticum) or page 44 (Additional Readings from Sacred Scripture), or from elsewhere in *Holy Communion and Worship of the Eucharistic Mystery outside Mass*, *The Order of the Anointing of the Sick and of their Pastoral Care*, or the *Lectionary for Mass*. Readings may also be drawn from the Mass of the day or of the nearest Sunday, especially for ongoing ministry to sick and homebound persons (cf. nos. 58, 71).]

A Matthew 8:14-17

Jesus entered the house of Peter,
> and saw Peter's mother-in-law lying in bed with a fever.

Jesus touched her hand, the fever left her,
> and she rose and waited on him.

When it was evening, they brought him many who were possessed by demons,
> and he drove out the spirits by a word and cured all the sick,

to fulfill what had been said by Isaiah the prophet:

> *He took away our infirmities*
> *and bore our diseases.*

Commentaries on the readings from Sacred Scripture in this book can be found in the appendix on pages 48–51.

B John 14:23

**Whoever loves me will keep my word,
and my Father will love him,
and we will come to him and make our dwelling with him.**

C John 15:5

**I am the vine, you are the branches.
Whoever remains in me and I in him will bear much fruit,
because without me you can do nothing.**

D 1 John 4:16

**We have come to know and to believe in the love God has for us.
God is love, and whoever remains in love remains in God and God in him.**

HOLY COMMUNION

59. Then the minister introduces the Lord's Prayer in these or similar words:

**Now let us together call upon God,
as our Lord Jesus Christ taught us to pray:**

And all together continue:

Our Father, who art in heaven,
hallowed be thy name;
thy kingdom come,

thy will be done
on earth as it is in heaven.
Give us this day our daily bread,
and forgive us our trespasses,
as we forgive those who trespass against us;
and lead us not into temptation,
but deliver us from evil.

60. Then the minister shows the Most Blessed Sacrament, saying:

**Behold the Lamb of God,
behold him who takes away the sins of the world.
Blessed are those called to the supper of the Lamb.**

The sick person and any others who will receive Communion say once:

Lord, I am not worthy
that you should enter under my roof,
but only say the word
and my soul shall be healed.

61. The minister approaches the sick person, and showing them the Sacrament, says:

The Body of Christ (or: The Blood of Christ).

The sick person replies:

Amen.

And receives Holy Communion.

Those present who wish to receive Communion receive the Sacrament in the usual way.

THE ORDINARY RITE

62.   When the distribution of Communion is complete, the minister carries out the purification as usual. Then, if appropriate, a sacred silence may be observed for a while.

Then the minister says the concluding prayer:

Let us pray.

A **O Lord, holy Father, almighty and eternal God,
with faith we entreat you
that the most holy Body (most holy Blood)
of our Lord Jesus Christ your Son
may benefit our brother (sister) who receives it
as an everlasting remedy
for both body and soul.
Through Christ our Lord.**

All reply: Amen.

Other optional prayers (cf. nos. 210, 211, 216):

B **O God, who have accomplished the work of human redemption
through the Paschal Mystery of your Only Begotten Son,
graciously grant that we, who confidently proclaim,
under sacramental signs, the Death and Resurrection of Christ,
may experience continued increase of your saving grace.
Through Christ our Lord.**

All reply: Amen.

C **Pour on us, O Lord, the Spirit of your love,
and in your kindness
make those you have nourished
by this one heavenly Bread
one in mind and heart.
Through Christ our Lord.**

All reply: Amen.

D **O God, who have willed that we be partakers
in the one Bread and the one Chalice,
grant us, we pray, so to live
that, made one in Christ,
we may joyfully bear fruit
for the salvation of the world.
Through Christ our Lord.**

All reply: Amen.

The Concluding Rites

63. Then the minister, while invoking God's blessing and signing himself (herself), says:

A **May the Lord bless us,
protect us from all evil
and lead us to everlasting life.**

All reply: Amen.

Or:

B **May the almighty and merciful Lord bless us
and keep us,
the Father, and the Son, and the Holy Spirit.**

All reply: Amen.

OUTLINE OF A SHORTER RITE OF COMMUNION OF THE SICK

THE INTRODUCTORY RITES

HOLY COMMUNION

THE CONCLUDING RITES

A SHORTER RITE OF COMMUNION OF THE SICK

64. This shorter rite is used when Holy Communion is to be given to a number of the sick in different rooms of the same building, for example, to those staying in the same hospital. As the case requires, some elements taken from the ordinary rite may be added (nos. 56–63).

The Introductory Rites

65. The rite may begin either in the church or chapel or in the first room, while the minister says this antiphon:

A O sacred banquet, in which Christ is received:
the memory of his Passion is renewed,
the mind is filled with grace,
and a pledge of future glory is given to us.

Other optional antiphons (cf. nos. 201–203):

B How delightful your spirit, O Lord!
To show your sweetness to your children,
you fill the hungry with good things,
offering them the sweetest bread from heaven,
and sending the rich and haughty away empty.

C **I am the living bread that came down from
heaven;
whoever eats of this bread will live for ever;
and the bread that I will give
is my flesh for the life of the world.**

66. Then the minister, accompanied by a person carrying a candle if appropriate, approaches the sick persons.

[As noted in no. 64, if there is time and it seems desirable, elements from the ordinary rite on pages 16–24 may be added at this point (for example: adoration of the Blessed Sacrament, a greeting, Scripture reading, or the Lord's Prayer). Added elements should not be so prolonged as to interrupt the integrity of this rite.]

Holy Communion

The minister then says once to all the sick who are present in the same room or to each of the communicants individually:

**Behold the Lamb of God,
behold him who takes away the sins of the
world.
Blessed are those called to the supper of the
Lamb.**

And the communicants add once:

Lord, I am not worthy
that you should enter under my roof,
but only say the word
and my soul shall be healed.

The minister approaches the sick person, and showing them the Sacrament, says:

The Body of Christ (or: **The Blood of Christ**).

The sick person replies:

> Amen.

And receives Holy Communion.

Those present who wish to receive Communion receive the Sacrament in the usual way.

The Concluding Rites

67. The rite is concluded with a prayer (cf. no. 62) which may be said either in a church or a chapel or in the last room.

> **Let us pray.**

A **O Lord, holy Father, almighty and eternal God,
with faith we entreat you
that the most holy Body (most holy Blood)
of our Lord Jesus Christ your Son
may benefit our brother (sister) who receives it
as an everlasting remedy
for both body and soul.
Through Christ our Lord.**
All reply: Amen.

Other optional prayers (cf. nos. 210, 211, 216):

B **O God, who have accomplished the work of human redemption
through the Paschal Mystery of your Only Begotten Son,
graciously grant that we, who confidently proclaim,
under sacramental signs, the Death and Resurrection of Christ,**

may experience continued increase of your
    saving grace.
Through Christ our Lord.

All reply: Amen.

C Pour on us, O Lord, the Spirit of your love,
and in your kindness
make those you have nourished
by this one heavenly Bread
one in mind and heart.
Through Christ our Lord.

All reply: Amen.

D O God, who have willed that we be partakers
in the one Bread and the one Chalice,
grant us, we pray, so to live
that, made one in Christ,
we may joyfully bear fruit
for the salvation of the world.
Through Christ our Lord.

All reply: Amen.

OUTLINE OF VIATICUM

THE INTRODUCTORY RITES

THE SHORTER READING OF THE WORD OF GOD

THE PROFESSION OF BAPTISMAL FAITH

PRAYER FOR THE SICK PERSON

VIATICUM

THE CONCLUDING RITES

VIATICUM

The Introductory Rites

68. Wearing vestments appropriate for this ministry (cf. no. 20), after approaching the sick person, the minister warmly greets them and the others present, using, if appropriate, the greeting:

A **Peace to this house and all here.**

Other words from Sacred Scripture, with which the faithful are customarily greeted, may also be used (cf. nos. 27 and 189).

> [If using a greeting with a response, the minister may find it pastorally helpful to add the response to the end of the greeting, and then invite all to respond.]

B **Bless the Lord, brothers and sisters,**
who in his goodness invites us (you)
to the table of the Body of Christ.

> All: Blessed be God for ever.

C **Grace to you and peace from God our Father**
and the Lord Jesus Christ.

> All: Blessed be the God and Father of our Lord Jesus Christ.

Then, after placing the Sacrament on a table, the minister and all present adore it.

69. Afterwards, the minister addresses those present with the following introduction, or another one more suited to the sick person's conditions:

> **Dear brothers and sisters,**
> **before he passed from this world to the Father,**
> **the Lord Jesus Christ left us the Sacrament of his Body and Blood,**
> **so that at the hour of our passing from this life to him,**
> **we may be strengthened by the Viaticum of his Body and Blood**
> **and be fortified with the pledge of resurrection.**
> **United with our brother (sister) in charity,**
> **let us pray for him (her).**

And all pray in silence for a while.

70. The minister invites the sick person and others present to take part in the Penitential Act:

> **Brethren (Brothers and sisters), let us acknowledge our sins,**
> **and so prepare ourselves to participate in this sacred celebration.**

A brief pause for silence follows. Then all recite together the I confess:

A
> I confess to almighty God
> and to you, my brothers and sisters,
> that I have greatly sinned,
> in my thoughts and in my words,
> in what I have done and in what I have failed to do,

And, striking their breast, they say:

through my fault, through my fault,
through my most grievous fault;

Then they continue:

therefore I ask blessed Mary ever-Virgin,
all the Angels and Saints,
and you, my brothers and sisters,
to pray for me to the Lord our God.

Other optional formulas of the Penitential Act
(cf. nos. 190–191):

B Minister: **Have mercy on us, O Lord.**
All: For we have sinned against you.

Minister: **Show us, O Lord, your mercy.**
All: And grant us your salvation.

C Minister: **You gained salvation for us by your Paschal Mystery:**
Lord, have mercy
Or: **Kyrie, eleison.**
All: Lord, have mercy.
Or: Kyrie, eleison.

Minister: **You never cease to renew among us the wonders of your Passion:**
Christ, have mercy.
Or: **Christe, eleison.**
All: Christ, have mercy.
Or: Christe, eleison.

(continued)

Minister:	**You make us sharers in your Paschal Sacrifice through the reception of your Body: Lord, have mercy.**
	Or: **Kyrie, eleison.**
All:	Lord, have mercy.
	Or: Kyrie, eleison.

The minister concludes:

May almighty God have mercy on us, forgive us our sins, and bring us to everlasting life.

All reply: Amen.

The Shorter Reading of the Word of God

71. It is very appropriate that one of those present or the minister read a brief text of Sacred Scripture, for example:

E John 6:54-58 (Shorter form, [ ], 6:54-55)

[Whoever eats my Flesh and drinks my Blood
   has eternal life,
   and I will raise him on the last day.
For my Flesh is true food,
   and my Blood is true drink.]
Whoever eats my Flesh and drinks my Blood
   remains in me and I in him.
Just as the living Father sent me
   and I have life because of the Father,
   so also the one who feeds on me
   will have life because of me.
This is the bread that came down from heaven.
Unlike your ancestors who ate and still died,
   whoever eats this bread will live forever.

F John 14:6

I am the way and the truth and the life.
No one comes to the Father except through me.

G John 14:27

Peace I leave with you; my peace I give to you.
Not as the world gives do I give it to you.
Do not let your hearts be troubled or afraid.

Commentaries on the readings from Sacred Scripture in this book can be found in the appendix on pages 48–51.

H 1 Corinthians 10:16-17

**Brothers and sisters:
The cup of blessing that we bless,
   is it not a participation in the Blood of Christ?
The bread that we break,
   is it not a participation in the Body of Christ?
Because the loaf of bread is one,
   we, though many, are one Body,
   for we all partake of the one loaf.**

[Readings may also be chosen from those that appear on page 20 or 44, or another reading chosen from *Holy Communion and Worship of the Eucharistic Mystery outside Mass*, *The Order of the Anointing of the Sick and of their Pastoral Care*, or the *Lectionary for Mass*.]

The Profession of Baptismal Faith

72. It is desirable that the sick person, before receiving Viaticum, renew his (her) profession of baptismal faith. Then, the minister having offered a brief introduction with appropriate words, asks him (her):

> **Do you believe in God,**
> **the Father almighty,**
> **Creator of heaven and earth?**
> ℟. I do.

Minister:

> **Do you believe in Jesus Christ, his only Son,**
>   **our Lord,**
> **who was born of the Virgin Mary,**
> **suffered death and was buried,**
> **rose again from the dead**
> **and is seated at the right hand of the Father?**
> ℟. I do.

Minister:

> **Do you believe in the Holy Spirit,**
> **the holy catholic Church,**
> **the communion of saints,**
> **the forgiveness of sins,**
> **the resurrection of the body,**
> **and life everlasting?**
> ℟. I do.

Prayer for the Sick Person

73. Then, if the condition of the sick person permits, a brief prayer takes place in these or similar words, with the sick person, insofar as possible, and those present responding:

**Dear brothers and sisters,
with one heart let us invoke the Lord Jesus Christ:**

**— To you, O Lord, who loved us to the end
and handed yourself over to death in order to give us life,
we pray for our brother (sister).**
℟. Hear us, O Lord.

**— To you, O Lord, who said:
Whoever eats my Flesh and drinks my Blood has eternal life,
we pray for our brother (sister).**
℟. Hear us, O Lord.

**— To you, O Lord, who invite us to that banquet
where there will be no more pain or grief,
neither sadness, nor separation,
we pray for our brother (sister).**
℟. Hear us, O Lord.

Viaticum

74. Then the minister introduces the Lord's Prayer in these or similar words:

**Now let us together call upon God,
as our Lord Jesus Christ taught us to pray:**

And all together continue:

Our Father, who art in heaven,
hallowed be thy name;
thy kingdom come,
thy will be done
on earth as it is in heaven.
Give us this day our daily bread,
and forgive us our trespasses,
as we forgive those who trespass against us;
and lead us not into temptation,
but deliver us from evil.

75. Then the minister shows the Most Blessed Sacrament, saying:

**Behold the Lamb of God,
behold him who takes away the sins of the world.
Blessed are those called to the supper of the Lamb.**

The sick person, if possible, and any others who will receive Communion say once:

Lord, I am not worthy
that you should enter under my roof,
but only say the word
and my soul shall be healed.

76. The minister approaches the sick person, and showing them the Sacrament, says:

The Body of Christ (or: The Blood of Christ).

The sick person replies:

Amen.

And immediately, or after giving Communion, the minister adds:

May he protect you and lead you to eternal life.

The sick person replies:

Amen.

Those present who wish to receive Communion receive the Sacrament in the usual way.

77. When the distribution of Communion is complete, the minister carries out the purification as usual. Then, if appropriate, a sacred silence may be observed for a while.

The Concluding Rites

78. Then the minister says the concluding prayer:

Let us pray.

A **O God, whose Son is for us the way, the truth and the life,
look lovingly upon your servant N.
and grant that, trusting in your promises
and strengthened by the Body and Blood of your Son,**

**he (she) may journey in peace to your Kingdom.
Through Christ our Lord.**

All reply: Amen.

Another optional prayer (cf. no. 223):

**B O Lord, eternal health and salvation
of those who believe in you,
grant, we pray, that your servant N.,
renewed by heavenly food and drink,
may safely reach your Kingdom of light and life.
Through Christ our Lord.**

All reply: Amen.

Then the minister says:

**May the Lord be with you always,
may he strengthen you by his power
and keep you in peace.**

Then both the minister and those present may offer a Sign of Peace to the sick person.

APPENDIX

ADDITIONAL READINGS FROM SACRED SCRIPTURE

[The following readings may be used in place of those given on pages 16-24 (Ordinary Rite) or 32-42 (Viaticum). They are taken from *Holy Communion and Worship of the Eucharistic Mystery outside Mass*, no. 157 and *The Order of the Anointing of the Sick and of their Pastoral Care*, nos. 167, 168, 172.]

1 Isaiah 49:13-15

A reading from the Book of the Prophet Isaiah

Sing out, O heavens, and rejoice, O earth,
   break forth into song, you mountains.
For the LORD comforts his people
   and shows mercy to his afflicted.

But Zion said, "The LORD has forsaken me;
   my Lord has forgotten me."
Can a mother forget her infant,
   be without tenderness for the child of her womb?
Even should she forget,
   I will never forget you.

The word of the Lord.

Commentaries on the readings from Sacred Scripture in this book can be found in the appendix on pages 48–51.

J Romans 8:18-27

A reading from the Letter of Saint Paul to the Romans

Brothers and sisters:
I consider that the sufferings of this present time are as nothing
 compared with the glory to be revealed for us.
For creation awaits with eager expectation
 the revelation of the children of God;
 for creation was made subject to futility,
 not of its own accord but because of the one who subjected it,
 in hope that creation itself
 would be set free from slavery to corruption
 and share in the glorious freedom of the children of God.
We know that all creation is groaning in labor pains even until now;
 and not only that, but we ourselves,
 who have the firstfruits of the Spirit,
 we also groan within ourselves
 as we wait for adoption, the redemption of our bodies.
For in hope we were saved.
Now hope that sees for itself is not hope.
For who hopes for what one sees?
But if we hope for what we do not see, we wait with endurance.

In the same way, the Spirit too comes to the
> aid of our weakness;
> > for we do not know how to pray as we ought,
> > but the Spirit himself intercedes with
> > > inexpressible groanings.
>
And the one who searches hearts
> knows what is the intention of the Spirit,
> because it intercedes for the holy ones
> according to God's will.

The word of the Lord.

K — Romans 8:31b-35, 37-39

A reading from the Letter of Saint Paul to the Romans

Brothers and sisters:
If God is for us, who can be against us?
He who did not spare his own Son
> but handed him over for us all,
> > how will he not also give us everything else
> > > along with him?

Who will bring a charge against God's chosen ones?
It is God who acquits us.
Who will condemn?
It is Christ Jesus who died, rather, was raised,
> who also is at the right hand of God,
> who indeed intercedes for us.

What will separate us from the love of Christ?
Will anguish, or distress or persecution, or
> famine,
> > or nakedness, or peril, or the sword?

No, in all these things, we conquer overwhelmingly
through him who loved us.
For I am convinced that neither death, nor life,
nor angels, nor principalities,
nor present things, nor future things,
nor powers, nor height, nor depth,
nor any other creature will be able to separate us
from the love of God in Christ Jesus our Lord.

The word of the Lord.

2 Corinthians 4:16-18

A reading from the second Letter of Saint Paul to the Corinthians

Brothers and sisters:
We are not discouraged;
rather, although our outer self is wasting away,
our inner self is being renewed day by day.
For this momentary light affliction
is producing for us an eternal weight of glory beyond all comparison,
as we look not to what is seen but to what is unseen;
for what is seen is transitory, but what is unseen is eternal.

The word of the Lord.

COMMENTARY ON THE READINGS FROM SACRED SCRIPTURE

[These commentaries correspond to Scripture readings A–D given in the Ordinary Rite (pages 20–21), readings E–H given in Viaticum (pages 37–38), and readings I–L given in the appendix (pages 44–47). They are provided here to assist the minister in pastoral conversations, as needed.]

A Matthew 8:14-17

Jesus the healer is also Jesus the Suffering Servant envisioned by the prophet Isaiah, the one who enters into the suffering experienced by every member of the human family. Just as Jesus enters the household of Peter and touches the pain of Peter's mother-in-law, so too is Jesus with us in our pain. He takes it upon himself and transforms us into a people who are always in relationship with him and with one another, in suffering and in care.

B and C John 14:23 *and* John 15:5

At his Last Supper, Jesus promised to abide with us as people who hold fast to his word, and urged us to remain in him, like branches on the vine. In Baptism, the love of God made its dwelling in our hearts, because Baptism grafts us into Jesus Christ, and we draw our life from his life. Even our weakness is turned into strength by the miracle of God's life in us, and the Eucharist keeps strengthening our union with the Lord our God. We live in Jesus and Jesus lives in us, helping us to produce good fruit—love, patience, repentance, thankfulness, peace of mind and soul. Whether we feel distant or close to God right now, may the Eucharist we receive be an experience of God's presence in Jesus Christ, the true vine, source of new life.

D 1 John 4:6

How blest we are to have the gift of faith! In faith we come to know how much God loves us, and this love of God continually renews and refreshes us. Holy Communion is a grace-giving sign of God's constant, faithful love. God's love is so powerful that it removes our sins, helps us bear suffering along with Christ, and overcomes death, so that we will be raised up in glory to live forever with God.

E John 6:54-58

Jesus always remains with those he loves, who have eternal life because of him. Jesus shares his life with us through his Body and Blood, spiritual food that brings the very life and love of God into our hearts. Jesus promises that when we receive him in Communion, he lives in us and we live in him, forever.

F *and* **G** John 14:6 *and* John 14:27

As he did at his Last Supper, Jesus says to us today that he is peace in our anxiety, and the way that leads to eternal life. The Lord who lived and died and rose to life again tells us that he is leading us step by step to the Father. The Body and Blood of Jesus heals us, pardons our sins, and gives us nourishment on the way. Jesus assures us that we will live forever with God, and our joy will be complete.

H 1 Corinthians 10:16-17
Each of us is a member of the Body of Christ, which we means we are full participants in God's love--in Christ's life, sacrifice, death, and resurrection. We are in active communion with one another, and indeed with the entire Communion of Saints through the generations. In the Eucharist, may we know our participation in the drama of God's love, today and forever.

I Isaiah 49:13-15
In the midst of illness and pain, we all seek comfort, whether we are old or young, the sick person or the heart-broken parent, child, sibling, or friend. Throughout our Scriptures, we hear stories of our God who never forgets a weary people, is at work seeking to comfort even through what seems to be the darkest of days, and takes joy in whatever songs of hope and praise they are able to summon.

J Romans 8:18-27
Sometimes during sickness people find it particularly hard to pray. They are tired or weak, and their concentration wavers. Frustration and sadness can move in. But God's Word tells us not to worry. The Holy Spirit prays in us—in a way we do not understand, but God the Father understands per-

fectly. So we can accept our weakened condition in peace and simply let the Holy Spirit express our hope, our love, and our most important needs.

K Romans 8:31b-35, 37-39

Physical suffering and weakness can play tricks on our mind. We think of many problems but can't do anything to resolve them. Sometimes the memory of past sins brings sadness or even fear of losing God's love. God loves us so much when we are tired and weak. And when we lose hope, God tells us not to worry—nothing can separate us from the love of Christ, who died for our sins, washing them away in the Blood of the Cross. Neither sickness nor death can take away God's love. Nothing can stop Jesus from loving us, forgiving us, and embracing us joyfully forever.

L 2 Corinthians 4:16-18

It is hard to believe that suffering and weakness can be very strong medicine. Since Jesus suffered willingly for our sake, the cross of suffering will always be a sign of God's saving love for us. When we unite our sufferings to the Cross of Jesus, we experience a spiritual power beyond human understanding. In union with Jesus, our cross leads us to new life, for ourselves and for others. The Eucharist recalls the powerful dying and rising of Jesus. It deepens our union with Jesus and becomes strong medicine to heal us.

RESPONSORIAL PSALMS

Psalm 23 (22):1-3, 4, 5, 6

℞. (1) **The Lord is my shepherd; there is nothing I shall want.**

Or:

℞. **Alleluia.**

> The Lord is my shepherd;
>> there is nothing I shall want.
>
> Fresh and green are the pastures
>> where he gives me repose.
>
> Near restful waters he leads me;
>> he revives my soul.
>
> He guides me along the right path,
>> for the sake of his name. ℞.
>
> Though I should walk in the valley of the shadow of death,
>> no evil would I fear, for you are with me.
>
> Your crook and your staff will give me comfort. ℞.
>
> You have prepared a table before me
>> in the sight of my foes.
>
> My head you have anointed with oil;
>> my cup is overflowing. ℞.
>
> Surely goodness and mercy shall follow me
>> all the days of my life.
>
> In the Lord's own house shall I dwell
>> for length of days unending. ℞.

Psalm 34 (33):2-3, 4-5, 6-7, 8-9, 10-11

℟. (9a) **Taste and see that the Lord is good.**
Or:
℟. **Alleluia.**

> I will bless the Lord at all times,
>   praise of him is always in my mouth.
> In the Lord my soul shall make its boast;
>   the humble shall hear and be glad. ℟.
>
> Glorify the Lord with me;
>   together let us praise his name.
> I sought the Lord, and he answered me;
>   from all my terrors he set me free. ℟.
>
> Look toward him and be radiant;
>   let your faces not be abashed.
> This lowly one called; the Lord heard,
>   and rescued him from all his distress. ℟.
>
> The angel of the Lord is encamped
>   around those who fear him, to rescue them.
> Taste and see that the Lord is good.
>   Blessed the man who seeks refuge in him. ℟.
>
> Fear the Lord, you his holy ones.
>   They lack nothing, those who fear him.
> The rich suffer want and go hungry,
>   but those who seek the Lord lack no
>   blessing. ℟.

Psalm 78 (77):3-4a and 7ab, 23-24, 25 and 54

℟. (24b) **The Lord gave them bread from heaven.**

> The things we have heard and understood,
>> the things our fathers have told us,
>> these we will not hide from their children:
> that they should set their hope in God,
>> and never forget God's deeds. ℟.

> He commanded the clouds above,
>> and opened the gates of heaven.
> He rained down manna to eat,
>> and gave them bread from heaven. ℟.

> Man ate the bread of angels.
>> He sent them abundance of food.
> He brought them to his holy land,
>> to the mountain his right hand had won. ℟.

Psalm 116 (115):12-13, 15-16, 17-18

℟. (13) **The cup of salvation I will raise; I will call on the name of the Lord.**

Or:

℟. (1 Corinthians 10:16) **Our blessing-cup is a communion with the Blood of Christ.**

> How can I repay the Lord
>   for all his goodness to me?
> The cup of salvation I will raise;
>   I will call on the name of the Lord. ℟.
>
> How precious in the eyes of the Lord
>   is the death of his faithful.
> Your servant, Lord, your servant am I,
>   the son of your handmaid;
>   you have loosened my bonds. ℟.
>
> I will offer you a thanksgiving sacrifice;
>   I will call on the name of the Lord.
> My vows to the Lord I will fulfill
>   before all his people. ℟.

Psalm 145 (144):10-11, 15-16, 17-18

℟. (cf. 16) **Lord, you open your hand and feed us.**

All your works shall thank you, O Lord,
 and all your faithful ones bless you.
They shall speak of the glory of your reign,
 and declare your mighty deeds. ℟.

The eyes of all look to you,
 and you give them their food in due season.
You open your hand and satisfy
 the desire of every living thing. ℟.

The Lord is just in all his ways,
 and holy in all his deeds.
The Lord is close to all who call him,
 who call on him in truth. ℟.